**KITCHEN CONNECTION
A FOOD, RECIPE, AND MINDSET JOURNAL**

By: Corrine DaCosta

dedicated to my beautiful child, family , and friends

Attention is a tool - a knife
It will be a blade to shape my life

craving, cutting, slicing, sculpting

Presence is an ingredient - secret sauce
It gives my life that unique seasoning

flavor, sabor, essense, aroma

Passion is the fuel - the heat source
I will not let myself be the extinguish the fire

flames, heat, warmth, pyre

The body is structure - cuisine
Influenced by culture, tradition, spirituality,
technique, ingredients, regionality, temporality

cookin', the entree', being a 'snack' ,nourishing

The mind is artistry - composed dish
Tying you together, taking energy and time to make it
satisfying, but it is always valuable and beautiful

We are knowledge embodied
We are edible gastronomy

# INTRODUCTION

Have you ever heard the phrase A-1 since day one? Like A-1 steak sauce? Yes!
Well you have had your own back your entire life. You are the master chef of the dish that is your life. The experiences that make up your recipe box are equal parts story and sustenance.

Think about a cherished family recipe. You know the one with the big vanilla spill on the side, three edges missing, and seven typos.

Some wisdom and a shift in perspective allows you to see that you are lucky to hold a piece of paper that someone you care about used. It could be you, or your great-great-great so-and-so. If it's handwritten recipe the writing style or event typos may tell you about their personality.

That trendy recipe you printed from the internet with a long ass blog post might have a time stamp of a special day for you.
If you don't have these particular scenes pictured I'm sure something came to mind.
You could even see this journal or the recipes it inspires as holding that value.

Everytime you make that connection to the past it is important and helpful. Why? The past can help us learn and heal, but also because no matter who we are, us humans have encountered some thangs. Whether it was having lost(or finding) your mind, withdrawing from experiences due to stress, being stifled, or lacking focus. To take it to the kitchen we've all been **burned**, **mixed up**, or **felt the fire** . Those events happened for a reason and the context could be explored and explained years later. That long ahhh-ha moment. I know it sounds cliche, but I offer that cliches are just misunderstood universal truths.

Every part of you matters, your- attention, presence, passion, body, and mind. You are a beautiful work of art.

Hardship, self doubt, and ultimately perseverance in whatever form that takes for you is a part of life and especially in kitchens of all kinds. The journey is hard, but worth it like a five star meal. I am proud of you because you overcame all the things that could have broke you like a hollandaise, but you made it! And now you are here for all to see the results. Healing in a whole new way, in the kitchen- gastronomically, to repair or strengthen your realtionship with cooking, food, and self.

"Things changed when I realized my history mattered, my story mattered. People who are not necessarily supported are starting to believe in the strength of their voice. Starting to come together as a community."

MASHAMA BAILEY
JAMES BEARD AWARD WINNING CHEF

# ABOUT

This book is a....
Place for Self-reflection
Place for Recipes
Place for Creativity
Place for Success
Place for Learning

The kitchen is the home within your home, where life is transformed and celebrations are centered. This book will offer new ways to connect with yourself, your family, and friends with a fresh frameworks to look at food.

Insight will be layered like seasoning throughout the text to help you think about cooking and connection gastronomically.

With mindfulness practices incorporated into your personal food systems a change to your relationship with food will be inevitable. Cooking, baking and food are all things that seem to take up so much of our mornings, noons, and nights, weekends and weekdays. So lets switch up the way we think about some things. Welcome to the coffee colored kitchen and the coffee colored crew.

## A NOTE ON HOW TO USE THIS BOOK

Use every part of this book, every corner of every page, because it is yours and you deserve to not limit yourself and your expression.
If you see one . . . ( eclipses) let your mind wander and your pen and paper be guided by your breath and thoughts.

Write a reflection on a page with a quote.

Write a poem on a recipe page,

Do YOU!

Do what you want with these pages, to get the most of them. That way they mean more to you as well.

In the Coffee Colored Kitchen we have five beliefs:

- Mind Your Mise and Mise Your Mind
    - get your mind right and focus on your station

- Find Your Flow
    - understand how you feel in your own body and channel that while you interact with the kitchen

- Handle the Heat
    - kitchen safety basics and stress management techniques

- Unleash Your Creative Concepts
    - learn some culinary basics to leverage your creativity for more healthful and enjoyable food

- Be Blessed and Highly Flavored
    - focus on layering seasoning and flavor, while expanding your palate to new flavors and texture

# MIND YOUR MISE-MISE YOUR MIND

*Mise en place - meaning everything in its place in French; A part of the kitchen language lexicon.*

From our coffee colored perspective we have heard so many aunties and uncles say- *get your mind right,* right. The advice often stops there, like okay Auntie can I get an actionable piece of advice or wisdom?

How can we organize our thoughts so that they are the most useful to us?

This is how we do (it):
First write a list of things you want to focus on that or projects that you want to accomplish. - this is your mental prep list or punch lists( so you can knock it out,see that =)

If when you take a breath or a second to think and a thought comes into your mind that is not on the list- you will neatly put it away somewhere until it is time to focus on that thought. Shoot even make a separate list, text yourself, start an email draft, sticky note- think about what works best for you. It is simple, but it very chef-like to make lists. They are often referred to as punch lists is hospitality as notes with that previous pun.

- practical tip - I know texting yourself may seem silly , but seriously try it. Imagine you are texting a different version of yourself or your inner self.  Leave the message unopened or open it right away keeping in mind that that is the place where your special thought lives until it is time to do the work on that idea. My therapist says it is totally normal.

Mind your mise- also meaning mind your station (business). For some this could mean a literal business, your family and most importantly yourself.
Check in with self before you say yes or no, even to help others. The good news is that once you mise your mind it is easier to mind your mise. You feel us?
And like anything it gets easier with practice, make this a daily part of your routine for the best results.

# THE MANTRA TO MISE MY MIND

"It is hard to imagine a civilization without onions."

JULIA CHILD
CULINARY ICON

# MENTAL MISE-PREP LIST

DRAW THE WAY YOU WOULD SET UP
YOUR KITCHEN WORK AREA AND MISE EN
PLACE FOR YOUR FAVORITE RECIPE

# The Kitchen Timeline
## Culinary School Approved Meal Prep Organization Chart

**All The Things I Need**

**What I Am Producing/Menu**

**Cooking Timeline**

0:00
:15
:30
:45
:00
:15
:30
:45
:00
:15
:30
:45
:00
:15
:30
:45
:00
:15
:30
:45
:00
:15
:30
:45
:00

**Equipment Needed to Succed**

"So here we go now,
Holla if ya hear me though,
come and feel me flow
The flow pro poetical with
skills only A vet'll know better
know where's the wetter flow
that's on point like decimals"

## NAUGHTY BY NATURE
FEEL ME FLOW

# FIND YOUR FLOW

You know when something just feels right. Like a part of your soul is happy in the moment you are in.
You feel like a boss, Beyonce, Jordan or Serena in your own way. It feels so natural, the moment something clicks or when you hit that new viral dance. That feeling can drive your internal fire.
Sometimes it is fierce like a bonfire.
Other times it is a subtle whisper, like a secret.
You can channel that same energy while cooking, find your flow. It takes practice but it will happen eventually.

in the kitchen this can feel like . . .

Kneading a dough and knowing by touch it is ready to rest.
Turning at the right angle and speed to open and close the fridge with an elbow or foot.
Knowing exactly where the spice you need is,
Grabbing it without looking.
Opening the top and shaking just the right amount in the pot in one smooth motion. It is taking up space and moving at a confident pace.

It is your body's response to being so present and calm in the moment, chefs and cooks often call this being in gear. It is a great feeling. Have you felt it? Would you like to?

But be mindful, your flow is your flow.
Like NWA and Naughty by Nature they don't sound the same, but they make you feel the music the way they want you to.

The same is true for you. If you make a great sauce, be the sauce boss! If pastries are your thing that is more than fine too, make sure you bring that Angela and Vanessa Simmons energy(iykyk).

So get to know yourself a little better, find what you are good at, you will know-you will feel it in your body. Keep in mind that finding your flow is easier when you have done the work of mise en placing, literally and mentally.

# WHEN I FIND MY FLOW...

# WHATS ON YOUR MIND?

"I'm always asking what's missing. I'm not out here claiming I'm changing the game. But I'm creating a new lane. Jay-Z has a line that says, 'Don't go with the flow. Be the flow.' So, in hip-hop, I'm just trying to be the flow. That's it."

## SYREETA GATES
YO STAY HUNGRY FOUNDER

BREAD

IS

LIFE

AND

SO

ARE

YOU

RECIPE:

PREP TIME/YIELD:

SUGGESTION:

INGREDIENTS:

METHOD:

RECIPE:

PREP TIME/YIELD:

SUGGESTION:

INGREDIENTS:

METHOD:

*Notes*

# THINGS MY BODY KNOWS...

# THINGS MY BODY KNOWS HOW TO MAKE...

# I AIN'T SORRY. I'M SAFE

We have all had our feet held to some type of fire, just ask Chaka Khan or the Old Kanye.

We can also think of our passions as an internal fire that drives us.
That fire, helps us to do the things we are destined to do. So many types of fires in the kitchen, that have to be managed property to achieve our goals safely, because the danger is real. Burnout is real too, avoiding that in the culinary industry is possible and with current positive trends it has become easier to talk through and manage. Taking those steps away from the line of fire, whatever that means for you (business, parenting, even school) get some space to reflect, refocus, and grow is difficult but worth it.

Safety is so important in the kitchen and here is the space where we will talk about that.

4 tips for a safer kitchen environment

## 1.Sharp knives, slow start

A sharper knife means a safer one. The less pressure and stress you are placing on the knife the safer and easier it is to cut. Another note on knife safety, the slower you cut the more precise you can be, get a rhythm ( find your flow) and then speed up as you get more practice. Think of every time you grab a knife an opportunity to practice safety. You can increase speed when you feel ready, take your time- curl your fingers. There is no rush to get knife skills it happens over time, you deserve to take the time you need to gain the skills you want.

## 2. Have a wet towel and a dry towel

The wet one helps you clean as you or be used to stabilize your cutting board. The dry one keeps you safe as you grab hot things. Have a spot for your dry and wet respectively or even color coordinate-one color for wet, one color for dry. In the industry we call these side towels.

## 3. When in doubt, wash it

This means your hands, fruit, a cutting board, kitchen surfaces- but NOT CHICKEN. I know I know, contrary to popular belief washing chicken increases your risk of contamination (but do you). When washing your hands take the chorus of your favorite song and hum along, and hold your hands like you are dapping yourself up then make a twisting motion.

## 4. Communicate Clearly

Part of working in a professional kitchen means working as a team and letting people know what you have and where you are going as you flow through work areas. Saying 'Behind you'-when you are moving behind someone, sharp/sharp knife-when you have a knife and are moving with it or 'on your right/left' -to avoid kitchen collisions. The more comfortable you are in your kitchen flow the easier this is. Even if you are alone in the kitchen communicating with yourself is important to keep you present,mindful, and safe. Again practice makes perfect.

# HANDLE THE HEAT

When the heat is on what do you do? The heat here is stress. We are talking stress management, and the way each of us does this are valid. The reasons we handle 'ours' may or many not explicable, and that is also okay. Life is full of stress much like the kitchen. It is not about eliminating stress, because that is impossible, but it is about how we handle the heat.
Both our passions and stressors can get us hot-we want to feed the flames of our passions and extinguish the power of our stressors.

How ?
Fan the flames of passion by creating a daily reminder of what drives you. Vision board, phone wallpaper, painting, etc
There are even apps for that.

Extinishg the power of our stressors with, things you know are good for you exercise, meditation, fresh air, and journaling. Taking the power away from intrusive thoughts by acknowledging them, but not dwelling on them. Naming things that struggle with can reduce their negative impact as well.

Eating what is good for you- and even eating what is good for your soul (but not necessarily your body, it happens and it is okay)

> If these things seem far fetch, look at them from a culinary perspective. We will frame them as gastro goals.

When you are cooking try to engage your muscles. Think about how the muscles move when you cook. It will not only work you out, but keep you more mindful of how your body moves in a kitchen-for your flow. You ever make pasta or bread by hand? Kneading = constant crunching (visualize your abdominals moving in your head and you will feel them engage)

Meditation- while you are stirring a sauce or pot let your mind wander for the two minutes and think about things that make you happy including the sauce you are about to eat ( make sure the sauce is not boiling or burning! Use a light simmer on low heat for this) visualize love being poured into the pot or shake some love in from a pretend container.

Journaling- write a recipe from scratch inspired by your thoughts or edit a recipe from the internet that you like. In the margins annotate it with memories, inspiration, or things you like about the recipe. Add what ways you would change it, or what flavors you would use instead.

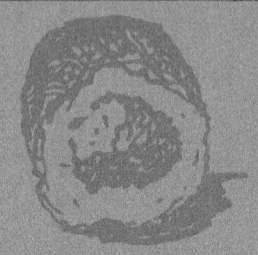

"As I traveled, I noticed that in every country, whether I was watching home cooks or professional chefs, and whether they were cooking over live fire or on a camp stove, the best cooks looked at the food,[...]the heat source. I saw how good cooks obeyed sensory cues, rather than timers and thermometers.

SAMIN NOSRAT
CHEF AND AUTHOR- SALT, FAT, ACID, HEAT

# THIS IS HOW I FEEL IN THE KITCHEN

# THOUGHTS WHILE I AM STIRRING THE POT

When it comes to Food
Color is Flavor
More Color
More Flavor

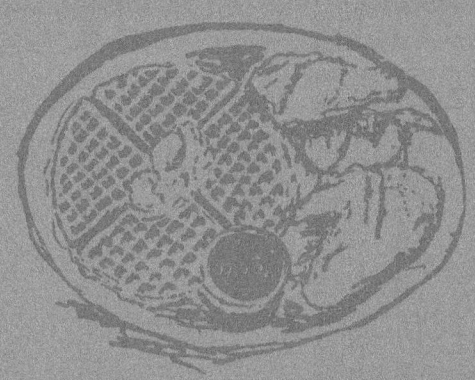

"You worry too much about what goes into your mouth and not enough about what comes out of it."

## LEAH CHASE
CHEF AND QUEEN OF CREOLE CUISINE

# IN YOUR MOUTH

What goes in and what comes out of your mouth that connects you to your body. Breath.

Our bodies are wonderfully made, period . When we breathe we exchange energy with all the life around us, and in us. The way the head is anatomically designed is rather fascinating. Your nose, mouth, and parts of your brain make up the olfactory system. This is the system that controls your sense of smell, and is connected to your limbic system. The olfactory bulb stimuli goes directly to amygdala and hippocampus, so the smells and flavor of food when you eat go directly to your brain. And all that happens with your breath.

The next time you smell your favorite food, I want you to take a deep breath, and try to smell deeper, smell something different. Record your experience here. The link between smell and flavor can be explored with a simple experiment. Use your index finger and thumb to close your nose, then take a bite of the food. Chew and swallow, then release your nose and repeat. This is partially the reason why when you eat with a cold your appetite isn't as prominent because food literally does not taste the same. So breathing in our opinion is an essential part of flavor development.

The Food(s)
_____
_____
_____
_____
_____
_____

First Smell Memory Activation
_____
_____
_____
_____
_____
_____

Second Deep Breathe Smell- What is something new you notice?
_____
_____
_____
_____
_____
_____

# OUT OF YOUR MOUTH

How you speak to and about yourself in your mind is what controls what comes out of your mouth.

An interpretation of what Chef Chase may mean with the quote, is not about how many calories does something have, but perhaps questions like where did it come from? who made it?( cause you don't eat everybody's potato salad) whose land produced this food? what intentions does this food have?

As a way to connect and reflect so you can enjoy what that mouth do. Did I get the best insta photo before I took a bite? Is organics better for me? Some of these concerns are vaild, but if they give you a lot of anxiety put it in a container and deal with it at another time. This is a great way to stay mindful, and 'watch your mouth' like everyone is always saying, however you are in control here and present which makes all the difference. You watch your mouth for you-not for others.

Write below any worries that come to your mind

_____
_____
_____
_____
_____

Now scratch them out

Focus on positive self talk cause -because you are always more than you think. Smarter than you think- kinder- capable- intuitive- better. And that negative voice in your head, is not even yours. You learned it from outside yourself, give it a name, you can talk back to the mean chef in your head.

Write something the mean chef in your head would say below

_____
_____
_____
_____
_____

Now scratch it out, as much as you need too.
And rewrite the script here.

_____
_____
_____
_____

## WHAT GOES IN MY MOUTH

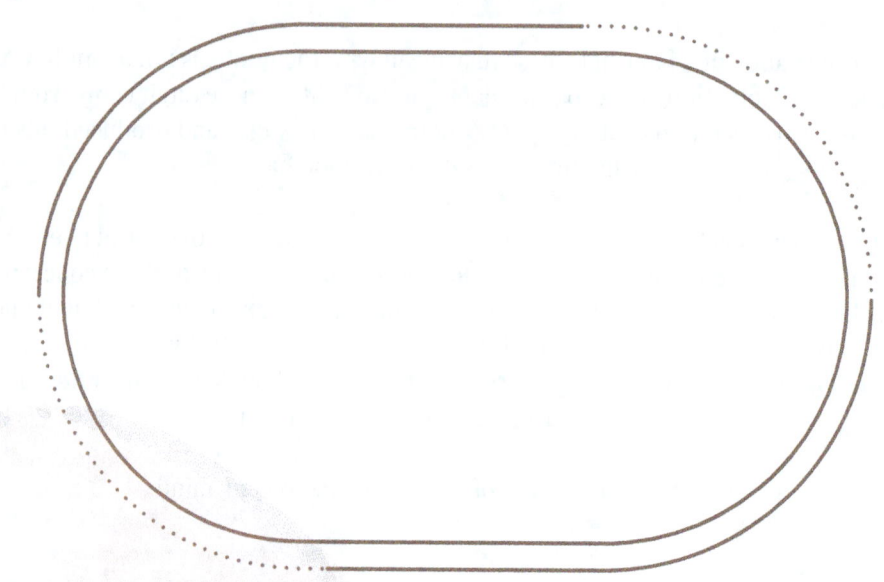

## WHAT COMES OUT OF MY MOUTH

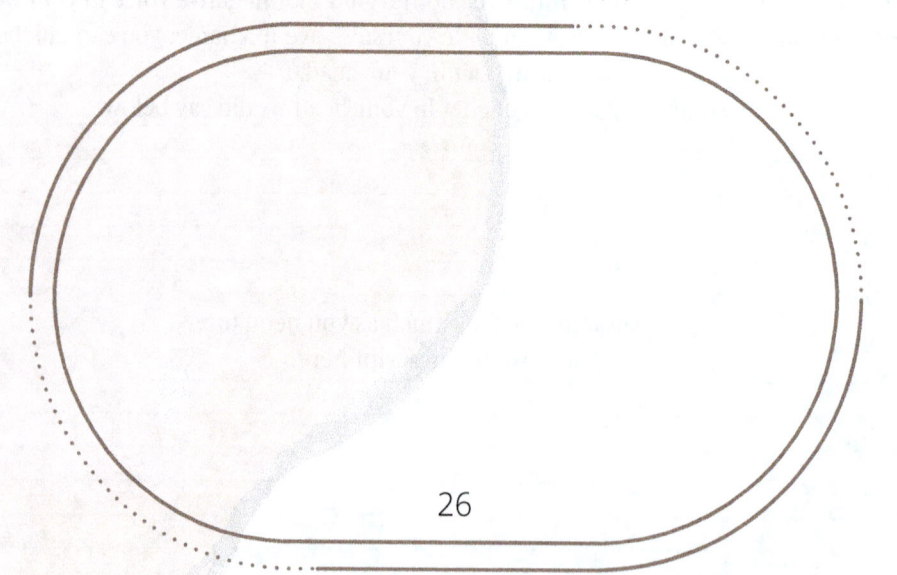

## WHAT MINDFULLY GOES IN MY MOUTH

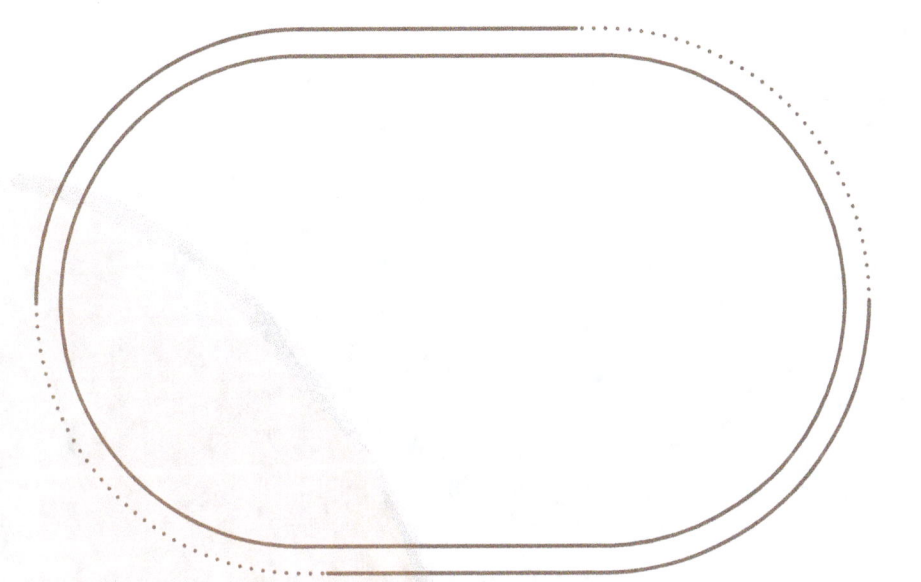

## WHAT MINDFULLY COMES OUT OF MY MOUTH

# In And Out

A part of me is in everything
I create
I am a part of every dish I
create

Are the best parts of me in
the recipe?

RECIPE:

PREP TIME/YIELD:

SUGGESTION:

INGREDIENTS:

METHOD:

RECIPE:

PREP TIME/YIELD:

SUGGESTION:

INGREDIENTS:

METHOD:

*Notes*

"I tell people all the time, you have to be in love with that pot. You have to put all your love in that pot. If you're in a hurry, just eat your sandwich and go. Don't even start cooking, because you can't do anything well in a hurry. I love food. I love serving people. I love satisfying people."

## LEAH CHASE
### QUEEN OF CREOLE CUISINE

# WHATS ON YOUR MIND?

# MY COMMITMENT TO ME IN THE FORM OF A RECIPE

I AM EVERYTHING.

I AM EVERYTHING
I CAN BE RIGHT NOW.

I AM EVERYTHING
I SHOULD BE RIGHT
NOW.

# UNLEASH YOUR CREATIVE CONCEPTS

Turning chaos into art is the at core of what drives every chef, or artist. Kitchens are messy and unruly just like our lives, but when you mise your mind, find your flow, and handle the heat, you operate at a higher level. You are able to see your passion or purpose everywhere, and thus are more open to all the good that life has in store for you.

Now moving from the proverbial kitchen to your literal one. Once you have an understanding of some kitchen basics, your creativity can be unleashed. Everyone has a creativity quotient, and if you think you do not, someone on our team can help you find it. Here is a list of ten kitchen basics to work on, to build up to ultimate creativity in the kitchen.

1. Basic Knife Skills
2. Egg Cookery
3. Pasta Making
4. Roasting Vegetables and Meat
5. Sauce Making
6. Baking basics
7. Soup/Stock Making
8. Cooking grains and legumes
9. Product Knowledge
10. Salad Building

You can get crazy with it. Look for inspiration everywhere. Coffee colored people have a legacy of innovation especially when it comes to food.
On social media or your browser bookmarks bar start a culinary creativity folder. Follow fun food hashtags, and look through your family recipe box and rethink an old favorite.
We highly suggest you practice the recipe before bringing it to any family gathering- learn from us!
You can use it as an opportunity to throw a little kick back. Have a R/D( research and development or recipe development ) night where you show off your hard work and get feedback. Then you can take a vote if you dish is cookout approved.

" The ability to see order in chaos, is called creativity

SIMON SINEK
MOTIVATIONAL SPEAKER

TODAY I KEEP IT REAL

I MAKE SOMETHING NICE

OR I MAKE IT TWICE

# UNLEASH YOUR CREATIVE CONCEPTS: CREAM OF WHEAT CUSTARD

Here is an idea we got inspired by a classic family breakfast, to pick up what we are putting down

Keep in mind creativity can also be expressed as versatility. For example using one item as multi-purpose ingredient for various dishes.

**Cream of Wheat Custard**
1/2 cup toasted cream of wheat or 2 cups leftover cream of wheat
2 cups heavy cream
2 cups milk
3 egg yolks
1/4 cup sugar
2 tsp powdered gelatin
1 tsp vanilla
1 tbsp bacon grease( optional)

toast or cook the cream of wheat according to package directions
(if toasting simply place the dry cereal in a dry saute pan and cook until brown and it is fragrant)
Then in a blender combine the cream of wheat, milk and heavy cream
blend until smooth
prepare the gelatin according to the package directions and set aside
once smooth add the cream of wheat mixture to a pot and bring to a simmer
whisk the sugar and egg yolks in a separate bowl set aside
remove the cream of wheat mixture from the heat and add the bloomed gelatin
temper the egg yolks and sugar by adding about 1/2 cup of the cream of wheat and mixing well
add the cream of wheat to the eggs a little bit at time (temper) to avoid scrambling
once both the cream of wheat and egg sugar mixtures are combined return to heat and cook over medium heat until the custard base is thick to coat the back of a spoon 2-3 minutes
remove from the heat and add additional flavorings
strain well and let cool


With the custard above you can make:
Ice cream
Creme Brulee
Panna Cotta
Cake filling
Banana or bread pudding

A good ol' google search can help you start to see the versatility of your prep and get you thinking in a way that is both practical and creative. When you open the fridge door, think like a chef creating a special. This mentality can be applied to food scraps and food waste for repurposing. This can save you money, time, and be better for the planetary health.

# WHATS ON YOUR MIND?

# UNLEASH YOUR CREATIVE CONCEPTS: MAKE AT HOME MUSHROOM MEAT

If you are looking to replace or reduce meat consumption in your diet we are proud of you-even if it is for one day a week. You would be doing so much good! Again keep in mind creativity can also be expressed as innovation based on necessity. The recipe below is for a meat alternative using nuts and mushrooms. If you do not like or are allergic to either, you can substitute either with your preferred swaps to make your dish a little more healthy. If you need a little help, feel free to reach out to any of the coffee colored crew for insight anytime. We got y'all.

### MAH Mushroom Ground 'Beef'
1 cup soaked, nuts of your choice
1/2 cup diced onion
4 garlic cloves
1 1/2 cup mushrooms of your choice
2 tsp kitchen pepper
2 tsp soy sauce
1 tsp liquid smoke( optional)
1 tbsp miso ( optional)
S/P to taste

Drain the nuts and reserve the liquid
Dice onions and add to food processor along with all the remaining ingredients, including the nuts
Pulse until the mixture reaches your desired consistency
If the mixture is to lose add more mushrooms or nuts
If moisture is needed add the liquid from the nuts*
*keep in mind that if you use salted nuts for this recipe the water will be salty so it means less work for you in terms of seasoning but a bit more mindfulness*

With the custard above you can make:
Tacos
Meatloaf
Bolognese
Sloppy Joes
Meatballs
Chili
Shepards Pie ( with a cauliflower topping for a bonus vegetable meal)

Again google or even some cookbooks can help you start to see the versatility of your prep and get you thinking in a practical and creative way. Take it from us you can impress people and save real coins this way.

THESE ARE THE CREATIVE MINDSETS I AM SHOWING MY HOSPITALITY TO RIGHT NOW.

IF I CAN'T USE IT NOW

IF I DON'T NEED IT NOW

I WILL TREAT IT LIKE AN INGREDIENT

PUT A LID ON AND SAVE IT FOR LATER

LIKE MY PREP

| RECIPE: | RECIPE: |
|---|---|
| PREP TIME/YIELD: | PREP TIME/YIELD: |
| SUGGESTION: | SUGGESTION: |

INGREDIENTS:

INGREDIENTS:

METHOD:

METHOD:

*Notes*

# "We eat for our stomachs, but we hunger with our hearts."

**PADMA LAKSHMI**
AUTHOR LOVE, LOSS, AND WHAT
WE ATE: A MEMOIR

# Where in your body do you feel knowledge?
## YOUR BODY KNOWS THINGS

# Be Blessed

THINK ABOUT WHAT
YOU KNOW

THINK ABOUT WHAT
YOU WANT TO KNOW

THINK ABOUT WHO
KNOWS YOU

"Find something you are passionate about and keep tremedously interesred in it."

"You never forget a beautiful thing that you have made,' [Chef Bugnard] said. 'Even after you eat it, it stays with you – always"

"To be a good cook you have to have a love of the good, a love of hard work, and a love of creating."

## JULIA CHILD
GASTRONOMY WOMANIST ICON

IPE:

EP TIME/YIELD:

GGESTION:

REDIENTS:

THOD:

RECIPE:

PREP TIME/YIELD:

SUGGESTION:

INGREDIENTS:

METHOD:

*Notes*

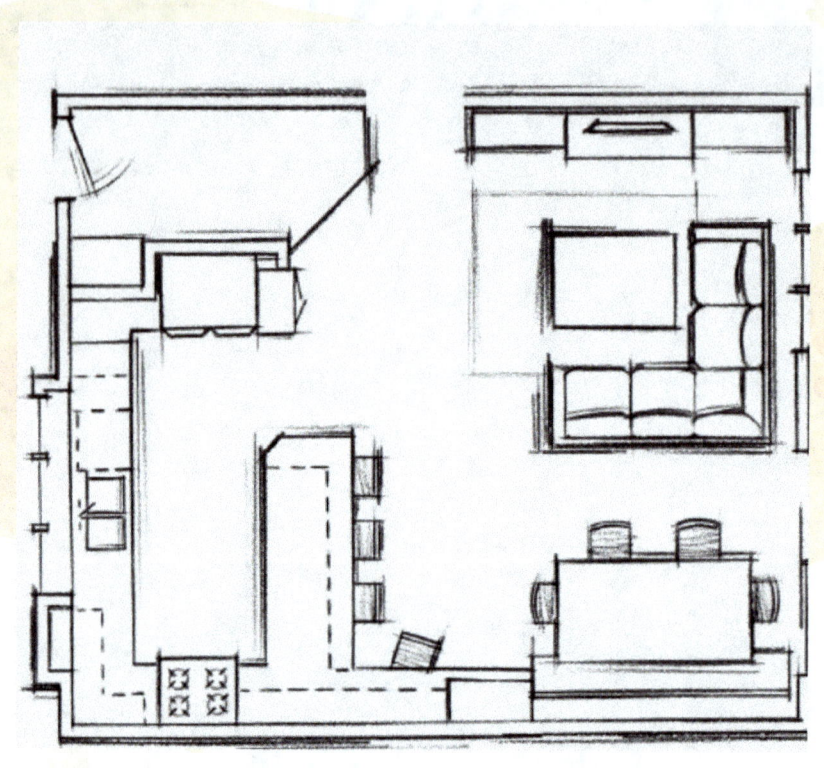

ABOVE IS AN EXAMPLE OF KITCHEN MAPPING. THIS IS A SETTING INTENTION AND BOUNDARIES EXERCISE. BASED ON A GASTRONOMY RESEARCH PROJECT. USING AN ANTHROPOLOGICAL METHOD ALSO KNOWN AS ETHNOGRAPHIC MAPPING IT IS USED TO HIGHLIGHT AREAS OF IMPORTANCE IN CULTURAL CULINARY SPACES.

DRAW A MAP OF YOUR KITCHEN. LIKE THE ONE ABOVE AND LABEL WHERE THINGS HAPPEN (THINGS TO CONSIDER: WHERE YOU DRINK COFFEE. WHOSE CHAIR IS WHERE AT THE DINING ROOM TABLE ETC.)

DRAW A MAP OF YOUR KITCHEN AND LABEL WHERE THINGS HAPPEN FOR YOU AND THOSE YOU CARE ABOUT. SEE THE PREVIOUS MAP AS AN EXAMPLE.

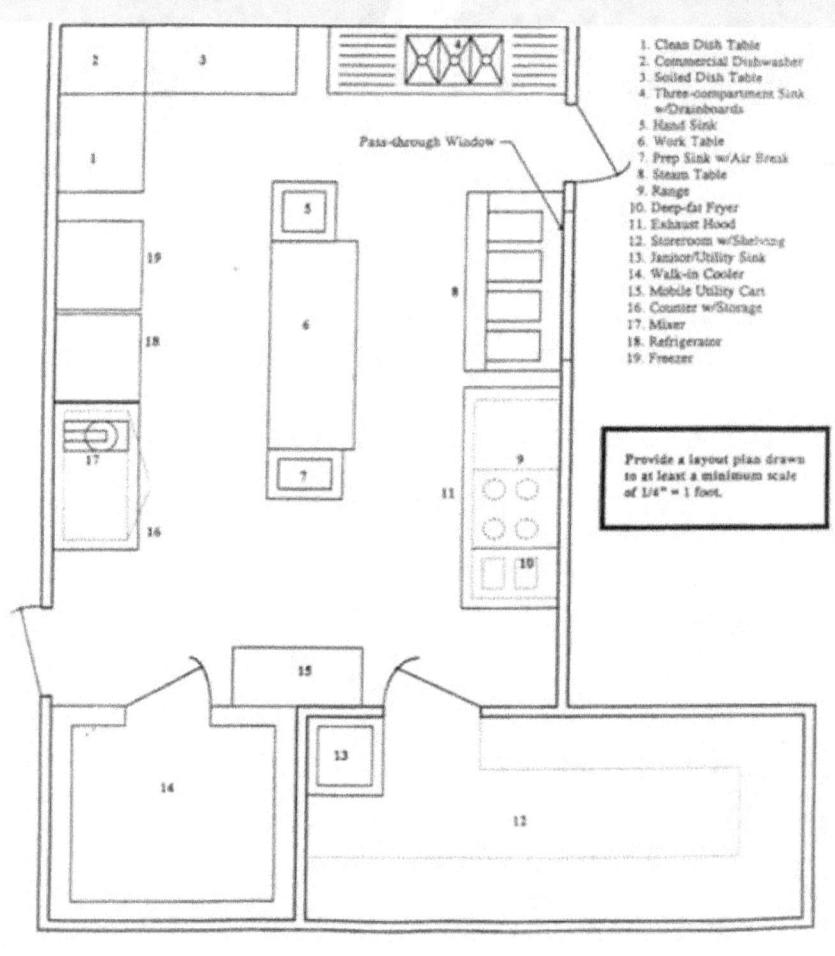

PROFESSIONAL KITCHEN MAP EXAMPLE

*THIS IS HOW I CLEAN UP THE MESS IN MY KITCHEN*

# "You Down With MSG?"

## COFFEE COLORED CREW

SATIRE BASED ON THE SONG OPP

# IF I HAVE TIME
# TO LEAN
# I HAVE TIME
# TO CLEAN

( A CLEAR AND CLEAN STATION REFLECTS A CLEAN AND CLEAR MIND)

RECIPE:

PREP TIME/YIELD:

SUGGESTION:

INGREDIENTS:

METHOD:

RECIPE:

PREP TIME/YIELD:

SUGGESTION:

INGREDIENTS:

METHOD:

*Notes*

"When aspiring chefs ask me for career advice, I offer a few tips: Cook every single day. Taste everything thoughtfully. Go to the farmers' market and familiarize yourself with each season's produce."

SAMIN NOSRAT
CHEF AND AUTHOR- SALT, FAT, ACID, HEAT

# BE BLESSED AND HIGHLY FLAVORED

Now that your creative mind is expanded, use it to think about flavor in a new way. First, let's talk about the flavor that isn't new to this, but true to this, **Umani**. Apart from being really fun to say, it is a taste modality that you have known your whole life. It is what makes tomatoes so tasty, or why ribs are so delicious and when you try to explain why you can't quite articulate it.

On your tongue you have receptors for umani, just like for sweetness, salt, or sourness.

Umami is mostly something called glutamates also known as( aka) MSG. You down with MSG? There is so much science on if it is good or bad. It is a lot to process, what I offer as being more important is how it makes you feel.

After eating it, how do you feel? Check in with yourself and eat accordingly. The stereotype that it is bad for you is unfounded and frankly based on prejudiced science.
I encourage you to use umani in deserts! Miso is a verstal ingredient that this applies to, also our favorite BROWN BUTTER!

Now a note on flavor... the more brown something is the more flavor it has... think about that =) but seriously it is science.

> The **Maillard reaction** is a chemical reaction between an amino acid and a reducing sugar, usually requiring the addition of heat. Like caramelization, it is a form of non-enzymatic browning. The reactive carbonyl group of the sugar interacts with the nucleophilic amino group of the amino acid, and interesting but poorly characterized odor and flavor molecules result. This process accelerates in an alkaline environment because the amino groups do not neutralize. This reaction is the basis of the flavoring industry, since the type of amino acid determines the resulting flavor.
>
> In the process, hundreds of different flavor compounds are created. These compounds in turn break down to form yet more new flavor compounds, and so on. Each type of food has a very distinctive set of flavor compounds that are formed during the Maillard reaction. It is these same compounds that flavor scientists have used over the years to create artificial flavors.
>
> The Maillard reaction should not be confused with Caramelization which occurs with sugars.

*Caramelization still counts as a browning of color, just with sugar instead of protein.

# BE BLESSED AND HIGHLY FLAVORED

You got the gist of the blessings of flavor, we will use this to think about layering seasoning, as well.

Layering seasoning into your cooking, is an almost instant way to level up your culinary practice. By salting and seasoning throughout the cooking process, at each step of a recipe, your finished product will be even more delicious. Adding a flavor at the beginning of cooking and the end for example, basil will add that nuance, because cooked basil and fresh basil are perceived differently.

The same technique to layer salt and seasoning, is also applicable to pairing flavors as well. Adding flavors that play nicely together, at each step or stage of a recipe enhances the dish. Bridging is also a great way to add that lil something, so cook with the wine that you will drink with your meal. It provides next level flavor, and is super impressive.
What is your flavor?


Careful with the salt, because that flavor will also intensify during cooking. There is a catch here, because salt ties all seasoning and flavor together, so be mindful. This is where tasting or as people I love say sampling is key.

And the next time someone calls you salty say thank you, because salt enhances flavor and brings out the essence of ingredients. So if the haters say you are salty they just aren't accustomed to your taste level, and that is fine, not everyone likes caviar and lobster, but those who do really enjoy them.


Using salt in the right way can make choosing foods that are better for your body easier. There are so many types of salt and the shape of the granules affects the way it seasons food. Making healthful things taste better = more healthful food choices- because we have mise en placed our mind and care and love ourselves(periodt) We eat what moves us in the coffee colored kitchen when we want to eat them; not because the mean (possibly fat phobic) chef in our mind told us we don't deserve this or we cant eat that etc. Easier said than done for sure, but we are working on it.

# BE BLESSED AND HIGHLY FLAVORED

Back to the **_FLAVOR,_** _lets reflect_

We added ours so you can get a feel for the exercise

Reflect on flavors you like
Example: Vanilla




Reflect on flavors you love

Example: Brown butter




Reflect on flavors that challenge you/ excite you/ scare you a little b
Example: Truffle




Now channel your inner Missy Elliot and flip it and reverse it.
Use flavors that scare you paired with a flavor you know you like.
Add umani to deserts.
Example: Old Bay sugar cookies. miso brownies etc.
When in doubt make it brown. Brown equals more flavor - cause it ju
makes sense. Taste makers have always been coffee colored or inspir
by those who were crafting cuisines while disenfranchised,
marginalized, oppressed, or enslaved. Making lemonade out of lemo
peels since before the great exchange, where do you think lemonade
came from-historically anyway.

I WANT TO WORK ON
CONSISTENCY

THE CONSISTENCY
OF ME
AS
THE CONSISTENCY OF
A SAUCE

# FLAVORS I LIKE

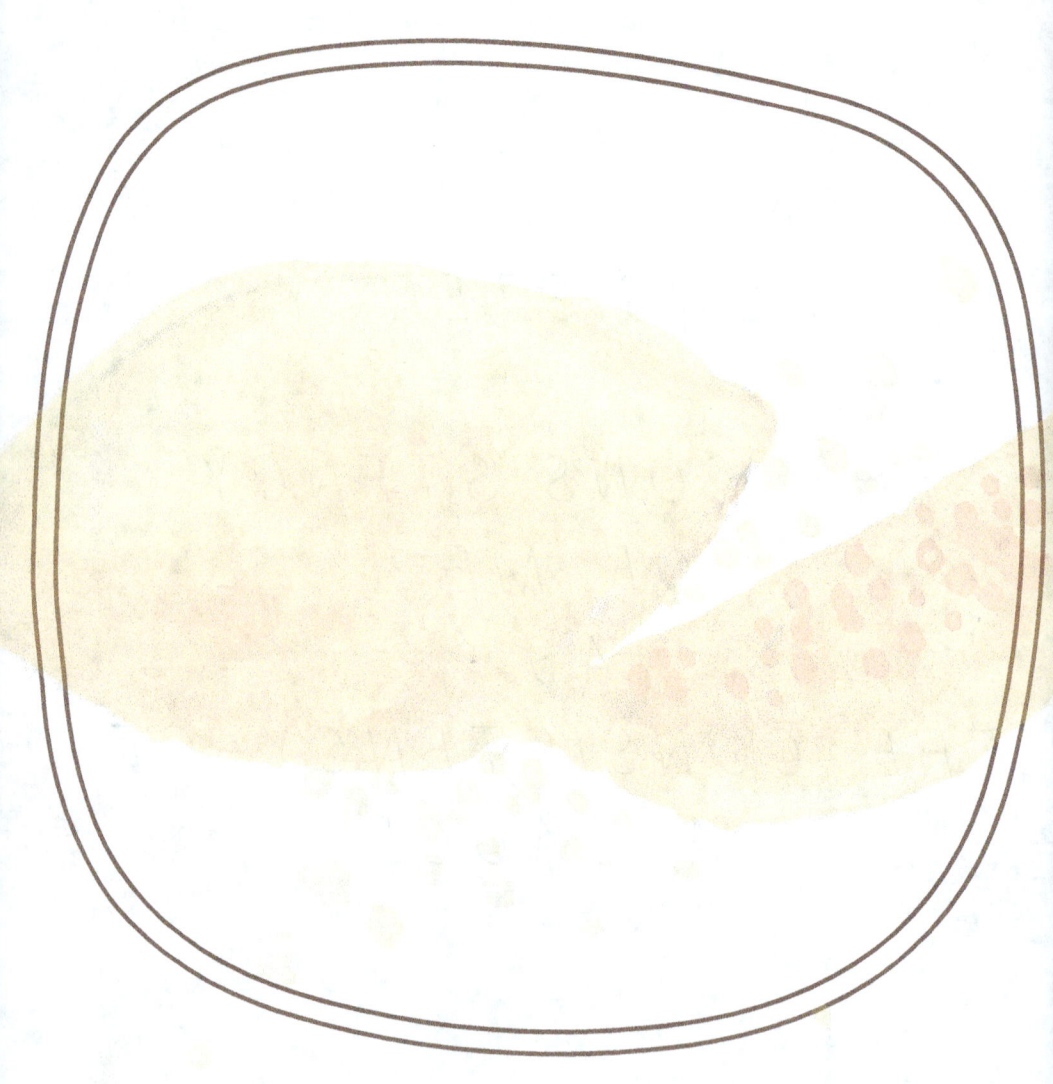

RECIPE:

PREP TIME/YIELD:

SUGGESTION:

INGREDIENTS:

METHOD:

RECIPE:

PREP TIME/YIELD:

SUGGESTION:

INGREDIENTS:

METHOD:

*Notes*

# Be Full

# Flavor

"There is no chef without a homeland. To be a chef today is to center yourself in the traditions of your roots and use them to define your art and speak to any human being about who you are; your plate is your flag. Many of our most pungent memories are carried through food, just as connections to our ancestors are reaffirmed by cooking the dishes handed down to us.

MICHAEL W. TWITTY
AUTHOR OF THE COOKING GENE AND CULINARY JUSTICE ACTIVIST

# FLAVORS I LOVE

ENVISION YOURSELF
MANEUVEING IN A
KITCHEN OR LIFE THE
WAY YOU WANT

CONNECT TO WHO
YOU WILL BE AND HOW
IT WILL FEEL

WHEN YOU MASTER
COOKING AND FOOD IN
A NEW WAY

. . .

WHAT DO YOU NEED TO
DO NOW TO BE THE
VISION YOU SEE?

# FLAVORS I AM CHALLENGED BY

# WHAT'S REALLY GOOD... TO EAT
## RECIPES

According to the internet an alternative spelling for this phrase it Wassgood.
Well, you learn something new erryday I suppose so. . . Wassgood? But there are so many meanings of this phrase in AAVE, pop culture, and slang. Based on inflection and tone it is up to you to determine the context and messaging behind the fun phrase.

This framework can be applied to recipes as well. Recipes are best with intent as food scholar and historian Michael W. Twitty points out. He even calls them spells in some of his works of writing. They are like advice, they work pretty consistently, take them with a grain of salt- do you trust the source?

For the coffee colored crew we like thinking about this in a more literal sense. What is actually pleasurable to consume based on our preferences, so recipes are a source of inspiration. In our kitchens we think of them more as a reference than a perfect science. Don't get us wrong cooking is science and baking even more precise like chemistry, but we are guided by our bodies, ancestors and spirit in addition. Which is what always makes things taste a little bit better( cue the memes).

So takeaways here, recipes are subjective, listen to yourself, and have specific intentions while cooking. Keep those intentions in the back of your mind while you work, it'll help more than you know.

The recipes we have included have suggestions to offer you guidance on how to think more like a seasoned cook. The recipes may be simple, but effective kinda like those universal truths we were talking about earlier, they are classic.

# WHAT'S REALLY GOOD... FOR YOU

## Roast Chicken

**TIME/YIELD:** 1 hour 15 minutes / 4-6 servings

**SUGGESTION:** nothing wrong with a good ol spice blend here

**INGREDIENTS:**
1 pre-salted chicken
6 tbsp. oil of choice
1 tbsp roasted garlic
1 whole lemon
1 tsp. salt
1 tsp. black pepper
1 tbsp. your favorite seasoning blend
or fresh herbs

**METHOD:**
Preheat the oven to 375 degrees
In a small bowl combine the oil, garlic, zest of the lemon, and seasoning
Place the pre-salted chicken onto a sheet pan lined with aluminum foil
Spread the flavored oil evenly onto the chicken and cut the lemon into thick slices and put into the cavity if roasting the chicken whole
If the chicken is in sections place the lemons onto the foil first and place chicken pieces on top
Bake in preheated oven for about 2 hours whole, and 30 minutes for cut chicken
Let chicken rest 10 minutes before serving

## Mashed Potatoes w/ Roasted Garlic

**PREP TIME/YIELD:** 40 minutes/ 8 servings

**SUGGESTION:** roast a few head of garlic at a time, very versatile

**INGREDIENTS:**
5 pounds potatoes
3 tbsp. salt- for water
2 tbsp roasted garlic
1 cup melted butter
1 cup dairy-
( milk, heavy cream, sour cream)
Salt to taste
White pepper if you are fancy

**METHOD:**
Preheat the oven to 375 degrees
To prepare roasted garlic take the entire bulb of garlic and cut where all the cloves meet
Place the bulb into a small piece of aluminum foil and pour about a tablespoon of oil over the garlic surface
Cove the bulb and put in the oven for about 40 minutes
Bring some seasoned water to a boil and then add potatoes
Taste until the potatoes are cooked
Once cooked, strain the potatoes and return them to the pot, dry the potatoes out by cooking on med. heat
When all the moisture has left the potatoes you can rice the potatoes if you have the equipment or stir your potatoes smooth
Then add your dairy, roasted garlic, salt, and butter.

## Sauteed Vegetables

**PREP TIME/YIELD:** 10 minutes / 4-6 servings

**SUGGESTION:** if using frozen thaw, and dry if possible

**INGREDIENTS:**
Boiling Water- depending on vegetable
Ice water
2 Bay leaves
4 lbs total of vegetable of choice
1 tbsp Roasted garlic
2 tsp. dried herb of choice
¼ cup oil of choice
S/P to taste

**METHOD:**
Put water on to boil and season with salt, and bay leaves
taste the water for seasoning
Blanch and dry vegetables with a clean towel
Heat oil in a pan on medium heat for 2 minutes
Check heat by carefully placing your hand above the oil
Once hot, remove the pan from heat add the vegetables and return the pan to the heat
Add the garlic, herbs, and a pinch of salt and pepper
Taste and adjust seasoning if needed

## Roasted Vegetables

**PREP TIME/YIELD:** 35 minutes / 4-6 servings

**SUGGESTION:** get creative with new flavor combinations

**INGREDIENTS:**
4 lbs total of vegetable of choice
1 tbsp Roasted garlic
2 tsp. dried herb of choice
¼ cup oil of choice
S/P to taste

**METHOD:**
Preheat the oven to 400 degrees
Mix the oil, garlic and herbs in a large bowl
Add the vegetables and mix again
Add a good pinch of salt and pepper, mix and taste
If the veggies make you smack your lips- you are good
Place veggies onto a sheet pan lined with alumium foil or parchment paper
Bake in preheated oven for 20 minutes, check color of vegetables, if deeper roast is desired keep in for another 5 minutes.
-Remember more color means more flavor

| RECIPE: | Simple Spicy Vinegrette |
|---|---|
| PREP TIME/YIELD: | 8 minutes / 1 cup |
| SUGGESTION: | great way to use up items in your fridge |

**INGREDIENTS:**

1 cup oil of choice ( olive if possible)
2 tsp. honey
2 cloves garlic, paste
¼ cup vinegar of choice
2 tbsp mustard
2 tsp. hot sauce
1 tsp. paprika
s/p to taste

**METHOD:**

On a cutting board place garlic and use the back of the knife to smash carefully
Add a generous pinch of salt and rub the salt and garlic together carefully with the heel of your knife and the heel of your hand
Place garlic and all other ingredients into a bowl or jar with tight fitting lid ( mason jar)
Whisk or shake the mixture to combine
Taste and add additional salt and pepper to taste

| RECIPE: | Simple Vinegrette |
|---|---|
| PREP TIME/YIELD: | 8 minutes / 1 cup |
| SUGGESTION: | balance the seasoning until you say wow thats good |

**INGREDIENTS:**

1 cup oil of choice ( olive if possible)
2 tsp. honey
2 cloves garlic, paste
¼ cup vinegar of choice
2 tbsp mustard
1 tsp. herb of choice
s/p to taste

**METHOD:**

On a cutting board place garlic and use the back of the knife to smash carefully
Add a generous pinch of salt and rub the salt and garlic together carefully with the heel of your knife and the heel of your hand
Place garlic and all other ingredients into a bowl or jar with tight fitting lid ( mason jar)
Whisk or shake the mixture to combine
Taste and add additional salt and pepper to taste

| RECIPE: | Seasoned Salad Greens |
|---|---|
| PREP TIME/YIELD: | 10 minutes / 8 servings |
| SUGGESTION: | always aim for something crunch, fresh, and sweet |

**INGREDIENTS:**

3-4 cups of salad greens of your choice
Fresh or dried herb of your choice
S/P to taste

**METHOD:**

Just before dressing the salad, tear fresh herbs or sprinkle dried herbs and toss
Start with 1 tsp of salt and pepper and taste
Increase salt and pepper according to your taste
*yes taste the salad greens for seasoning, I know it may seem silly but if they are delicious at this point just image the taste with the dressings

| RECIPE: | Quick Pan Sauce |
|---|---|
| PREP TIME/YIELD: | 10 minutes/ 1/2 cup sauce |
| SUGGESTION: | layoring flavor is key here |

**INGREDIENTS:**

1 tablespoon oil (or pan drippings)
1 whole shallot, minced
minced garlic, to taste
1/4 cup flavorful liquid of choice
* cough cough, wine if you wish*
1 cup stock of choice
2 tablespoons butter or a splash of cream
1 1/2 teaspoons cornstarch, slurry or flour roux

**METHOD:**

Remove the protein you have seared from the sauce pan
If enough fat remains do not add oil, add garlic and shallots
Sauté untill translucent
if at this point more fat is needed add some oil sparingly
Deglaze the pan with the flavorful liquid, reduce about a minute
Then add stock of choice and reduce 5 minutes
Mount (melt and combine) the sauce by adding butter or cream
Check sauce consistency if needed add the slurry or roux, if not taste and adjust seasoning with salt and pepper

## Brown Butter Blondies

**PREP TIME/YIELD:** 25 minutes / up to 16 servings

**SUGGESTION:** add crushed vanilla wafers, and serve with cream

**INGREDIENTS:**

1 cup  all-purpose flour
¼ tsp. salt
¾ cup (1½ sticks) unsalted butter
1 cup (packed) dark brown sugar
1 cup mashed banana
2 tbsp peanut butter( optional)
1 large egg
1 tsp. vanilla extract
1 tsp.  cinnamon

**METHOD:**

Preheat the oven to 350 degrees
Line a pan with parchment paper and cooking spray
Melt butter and banana in a saute pan until brown (3 mins)
Add brown butter mix and brown sugar into a bowl and whisk
Then add the eggs and beat until mixture is smooth and sugar dissolves
Mix flour, salt, vanilla and cinnamon and mix well
Bake in preheated oven for 15-18 minutes
Cool, and cut into desired shapes

## Chocolate Chip Cookies

**PREP TIME/YIELD:** 15 minutes / 16 servings

**SUGGESTION:** brown the butter, add your favorite warm spice

**INGREDIENTS:**

1½ cups  all-purpose flour
¾ tsp. (4 g) Morton kosher salt
¾ tsp. (4 g) baking soda
¾ cup (1½ sticks) unsalted butter
1 cup (packed) dark brown suga
¼ cup granulated sugar
2 large eggs
2 tsp. vanilla extract
1 cup chocolate chip

**METHOD:**

Preheat the oven to 375 degrees
Melt butter in a saute pan until brown (3 mins)
Add butter and sugars into a bowl and whisk to combine
Whisk enough air so that the mixture cools and is thick
Then add the eggs and beat until mixture is smooth and sugar dissolves
Mix flour, baking soda, and salt  together in a separate bowl before adding to the sugar mixture
Fold in chocolate chips and additional flavoring
Onto a baking sheet, scoop with ice cream scoop for even cookies- if time chill dough
Bake in preheated oven for 12 minutes

## Notes

"One of the greatest pleasures of my life has been that I have never stopped learning about Good Cooking and Good Food."

EDNA LEWIS
CELEBRATED AMERICAN CHEF OF THE SOUTH

# LETTUCE WRAP IT UP

How is all of this going to help? Now we understand the feelings towards therapy within certain cultural perspectives is not the greatest. In an episode of the tv series Black-ish Dre, the modern black father, makes a comment to his son- if I only believed in therapy.

Media mentions like this bring to light the stigma of mental health practices in communites of color, which is due. Many medical institutions were not designed to serve the needs of poc communities when a lot of their anxieties have been ostracized. As more mental health professionals that mirror bipoc people in hue, tone, and lived experience enter these institutions and take up the space they deserve, this makes the journey towards healing more feasible. These efforts are part of the movement that is quickly changing the negative perceptions of certain mental health practices to positive ones. Access is an issue within the food system and mental health landscape as well. Technology has made more equitable access to food and tools like therapy more practical and appealing, but there is still work to be done.

Within the Coffee Colored Kitchen we would like to offer another approach that may bridge the gap for mental health for our families and chosen families. We see cooking and baking as everyday opportunities to make mental health actionable with mindfulness.

You gotta eat, and lots of people enjoy cooking and baking for the exact reasons laid out my mental health professionals. By layering meaning through mindfulness practices and spirituality we enrich these practices and add more significance to an activity that already means so much to so many of us.

# LETTUCE WRAP IT UP

Checking in with yourself to be present while in the kitchen is a great opportunity to connect with self using food as a tool for healing. Eating and cooking mindfully keeps you in the moment and focusing on the intention of your actions and how those actions can create more pleasurable experiences for you and those you love.

Gastronomy is the study of how food shapes and connects us a people and thus society, I believe with the integration of mental health -via Culinary art 'therapy' food can be used as a tool for healing in so many ways ofter than just physical.

Cooking is a creative act and studies show that using your brain in any creative capacity for just a few minutes a day builds gratitude and more positive psychological pathways. I don't know who could not use more of those, right?

*'Art therapy is used to improve cognitive and sensorimotor functions, foster self-esteem and self-awareness, cultivate emotional resilience, promote insight, enhance social skills, reduce and resolve conflicts and distress, and advance societal and ecological change'*
*-American Art Therapy Association*

Marginalized people have always used art as therapy before there was a term for it. Healing the generational pains of the past with music, dance, and even entrepreneurship. Cooking is no different- taking what is given to you and making it immensely better with creativity and passion. They did it then and you do it too, now you are just able to articulate it in a different way- like a chef. I trust that you see and use this book to reorganize your mind, find your flow, better manage the heat, cherish your creativity, and be even bolder and more flavorful than ever.

Bless Up and Stay Sharp!

# SOURCES

"About Art Therapy." American Art Therapy Association, 2020, arttherapy.org/about-art-therapy/.

Atyeo, Kelly. "Chill Out with Chicken." Chicken.ca, www.chicken.ca/health/view/116/chill-out-with-chicken.

Charnas, Dan. "For A More Ordered Life, Organize Like A Chef." NPR, NPR, 11 Aug. 2014, www.npr.org/sections/thesalt/2014/08/11/338850091/for-a-more-ordered-life-organize-like-a-chef.

Conner, Tamlin S., et al. "Everyday Creative Activity as a Path to Flourishing." The Journal of Positive Psychology, vol. 13, no. 2, 2016, pp. 181–189., doi:10.1080/17439760.2016.1257049.

Farmer, Nicole, et al. "Psychosocial Benefits of Cooking Interventions: A Systematic Review." Health Education & Behavior, vol. 45, no. 2, Apr. 2018, pp. 167–180, doi:10.1177/1090198117736352.

Olfactory recognition: a simple memory systemBY P BRENNAN, H KABA, EB KEVERNESCIENCE30 NOV 1990 : 1223-1226

Sørensen, Lone Brinkmann, et al. "Weight Maintenance Through Behaviour Modification: With a Cooking Course or Neurolinguistic Programming." Canadian Journal of Dietetic Practice and Research, vol. 72, no. 4, 2011, pp. 181–185., doi:10.3148/72.4.2011.181.

Vaughnon, Shamontiel. "Dr.Michael M. Kocet, New TCSPP Faculty, Explores Culinary Therapy." Insight Digital Magazine, 21 June 2019, www.thechicagoschool.edu/insight/from-the-magazine/michael-kocet-culinary-therapy/.

"What Is the Maillard Reaction?" What Is the Maillard Reaction, www.scienceofcooking.com/maillard_reaction.htm.

## **ACKNOWLEGEMENTS**

I would like to acknowledge and thank first God (universe, spirit, and my ancestors) because, they are the reason I see things they way I do.
They are the ultimate creative force and I am so blessed to have the faith to follow the path they have set before me.
I also ask they continue to give me the strength no matter what to continue on his path for me, and my family to bring my passion projects to fruition.


 All the friends I consider family as well. Thank you for listening, being patient with me and guiding me through this journey, just as my family does.
This is especially true for my Mother-Nocola, father-Quincy, and grandparents Barbara and Nace, and brother Quinten.
My Cuñadas and Cousisters- I love you ladies so much!

My friends Roshara, Lauren, Khori, Nicole, Arielle, Liam, Jerrelle, Laurel, Rachel, and so many more- you know you are are, you are feeling it as you read this.

And SP you changed by life with a phone call and I am so proud to be a Woman Who Heals, you came into my life at the perfect time and make it so much better instantly.Consider this work a glowing review for Dr. Shawntres Parks and her services

# THANK YOU

I want to thank you for reading this and welcome you to the coffee colored crew. The community we are building is all about learning, growing, sharing, and betterment through cooking and gastronomy. That does sound like you doesn't it!
Happy to have you. We work with each other side by side- shoulder to shoulder, (and even virtually) just as we would in a kitchen to get things done to make a difference, no matter how big or small. You are incredible and we hope this journal has helped you in some way.

## AUTHORS NOTE

Hospitality is my legacy, teaching is my purpose, learning about food is my passion. When I was three years old I saw how food had the potential to bring people joy. I was taking orders from my great grand parents to cook on my wooden kitchen play set. As I grew older I got to help in the garden. The Piscataway land that they called home was magical. A true homestead, it had a grape vine, raised garden beds of strawberries, and a big green workshop. James Forrest Sr. was great in so many ways including being my (great) grandfather. He was a light-skinned man of statuesque build that loved the land. Most often seen in overalls, he was a fixer before Olivia Pope. He worked for the local telephone company, but he was the true message. I was blessed to have him in my life for long enough for him to teach me to respect everyone and everything, and work hard and be nice. That advice has taken me far in the culinary industry, to my limits and beyond. I thought food was the our connection, but the true connection between us was the love of the land and helping others. Our family intonation being 'its nice to be together' which we chant before each meal. Would you like to join my extended family? I'd love to have you!
Best, Corrine
@cori_rine26 on instagram

www.ingramcontent.com/pod-product-compliance
Lightning Source LLC
LaVergne TN
LVHW021601070426
835507LV00015B/1901